GOOD DOG!

GOOD DOG!

POSITIVE DOG TRAINING TECHNIQUES

DEBORAH WOLFE

POLESTAR
SIRIUS BOOKS

GOOD DOG!

Polestar Book Publishers acknowledges the support from the publishing programs of the Canada Council, the British Columbia Ministry of Small Business, Tourism and Culture, and the Department of Canadian Heritage.

Cover photographs by Lionel Trudel
Cover design by Jim Brennan
Printed in Canada

The cover: Thanks to the good dogs and their owners for their patience and understanding during our photo shoot, and our apologies to those who didn't make it into the final shot. Clockwise from centre: Sammy (on lap), Deborah, Taylor, Spook, Rudi, Chopper, Winnie and Lou. Special thanks to Spook, who appears as Bandit, and Winnie, who appears as Goldie, for working so hard to look like bad dogs. The puppy on page 113 is Belle Amie.

Thanks to Lionel for your calm and skill behind the camera, and to Morgan and Susan for your acting skills. Our gratitude also goes to Dr. Jack Brondwyn who provided information and feedback for the health care chapter, and Dr. Tracy Cornish who offered many useful comments on the text. You're all good dogs!

CANADIAN CATALOGUING IN PUBLICATION DATA
Wolfe, Deborah, 1966-
   Good dog!
ISBN 1-896095-17-8
   1. Dogs—Training. I. Title.
SF431.W64 1996   636.7'0887   C96-910417-0

Polestar Book Publishers
1011 Commercial Drive, Second Floor
Vancouver, BC
Canada   V5L 3X1
(604) 251-9718

10 9 8 7 6 5 4 3 2 1

ACKNOWLEDGEMENTS

I want to thank my parents, Barbara and Alfred Magerman, for giving me Standard Poodles to grow up with, and being great models for responsible care-giving and love. I also want to thank them for their flexibility and understandng when I left a career in law to return to my work and my passion for dogs. Special mention goes to Mike, my Number One dog, who has protected me more than once and has been a good sport about all of the Perfect Pet Care dogs who have shared his home and his human. I also want to thank Su T. Fitterman, my partner at Doggone Creative, whose wit and reliability have turned my writings into books.

GOOD DOG!

Preface

My love for animals has led to my career. Over the past thirteen years, I have worked hands-on with hyenas, mountain lions and, of course, many, many dogs. I am constantly amazed by dogs. They are experts at sensing human thoughts and moods, and at reading human physical cues like body language or posture. They can understand huge numbers of words, commands and human concepts, as well as communicate with other dogs world-wide.

People and dogs have a long history. The partnership works. Dogs are opportunists and survivalists, but they are also creatures of emotion. Their association with people gives them food, shelter, a defined role in a defined pack, and love; in return, people gain a love beyond their own capacity for strength and loyalty.

As the founder and principal trainer of Perfect Pet Care, I have dealt with hundreds of dogs and I have yet to meet a dog that is impossible, bad or mean. All dogs want to be good dogs. Each dog I've met is trainable, but sometimes a family and dog are a poor match. All family members must learn to take control and communicate effectively in order to teach a dog to fit into their lifestyle. Often, I go into a home of chaos and destruction, with torn wallpaper, shredded magazines, urine-stained carpets and owners who can't take it anymore. Other times, I'm called in because a pet has lost a limb or has gone blind and isn't adjusting to the new

GOOD DOG!

situation. I talk with the owners, get a full history, observe the dog and begin the work of teaching it trust and good behaviour with lots of patience and praise. After an increase in exercise, consistency, discipline, control and praise, we have a dog who is satisfied with himself, well-exercised, well-behaved and proud, as well as a family that is active, strict, consistent and who think its dog is the best dog ever. Doggone it, my job is done.

All dogs want to be good dogs. You can teach your dog good manners by following this easy training guide. By incorporating the training this book offers into everyday life, you will find that your dog is a source of pleasure, instead of frustration. There's no secret formula: rather than raging about and punishing bad behaviour, you'll learn to focus on and praise good behaviour. Before long, *your* dog will be a good dog.

LEADERSHIP

Dogs are designed to live in large groups with clear rules and consistent enforcement. They are taught at an early age to respect the leaders of the pack. This is the lesson a pup receives the first time it jumps up or annoys an older dog. The reaction is harsh, swift, painless but scary, and the pup learns fast. As your dog's teacher, you must be consistent and clear and you must always enforce your commands and rules. If you are a strong leader, giving directions consistently and clearly, your dog will accept you as leader and learn well from you. If you are weak, or do not give enough direction, he will fill the void by giving directions and enforcing his will. Your dog cannot live in a leaderless, "everyone is equal" collective.

A pack must always have a purpose and a leader. Most dogs are happy to have you as their leader, providing you prove yourself worthy. Become the leader by giving clear instructions and always enforcing them. Ensure there are consequences to defying or ignoring your commands. Use your body to back up your words. When you call, do it once, then walk briskly to back up your command and show that you mean business. If your dog indirectly challenges your leadership by stalling or responding slowly to certain commands, practice those same commands in a more controlled setting. Situations which allow him to ignore or defy you teach that he is the leader. Control him until he has learned to respond to you.

TOUCH

Touch is vital when training a dog. He craves it. Use touch as a reward that is earned by good behaviour and avoid rewarding bad behaviours with it. For example, a dog that jumps up during greetings should be redirected to sit and rewarded with touch only after he complies.

Touch is also crucial to a dog's healing. When a dog undergoes a dramatic physical change, such as loss of a sense or limb or the loss of his owner, touch will heal him faster and help him to adjust emotionally to the change.

Think back to the worst dog you ever met. Maybe he was a biter or a barker or a jump-all-over-you dog. Maybe he was an escape artist or a fighter or a leg humper. Imagine living with that dog in your home each and every day.

Dogs can be heroic, gentle, kind, playful and loyal. The same dogs can be aloof, defiant, destructive, aggressive and territorial. With a badly behaved, untrained dog, your day could go like this:

Diary of a depressed dog owner

7:00am	Woke up to whining and scratching sound. (It's Saturday — I could have slept in.)
7:30am	Stepped in warm pee spot on carpet outside bathroom.
7:35am	Let Goldie outside. She barked at the neighbour so I called her back in.
7:40am	Ran outside in my housecoat to catch Goldie who is barking her head off and snarling.
7:50am	Chased, then finally caught Goldie and dragged her back into the house.
7:55am	Gave Goldie her breakfast in the kitchen, went to take shower.
8:10am	After shower, I stepped in warm pee spot again. Cleaned it up.
8:20am	Dressed in crummy clothes to take Goldie for a walk.

8:25am	Goldie dragged me from tree to tree. I dragged her home.
8:45am	Confronted by torn-up throw rug and pile of poop near the fridge.
8:50am	Scrubbed first pee spot and dog spots again.
9:00am	Sprayed air freshener, lit incense and opened windows. Watched Goldie steal the rags and drag them across the carpet.

This could be you.

Or, you can train your dog. It takes time and effort — and commitment — but of course it will be worth it.

Why dogs dig school

Dogs are pack animals. They crave life with others. Dogs want and need to fit into the human family pack in a productive way. As well, all dogs, no matter how little or how lazy, need daily exercise. Ideally, they need exercise twice each day, time with people, mental challenges and stimulation through games, training or outings, and a job to do. Jobs range from retrieving to protecting and can even include gimmicky tricks like sing, speak, dance, or high-five. Without the challenges that communication and learning from humans create, dogs become bored. Bored dogs become destructive, and destructive dogs are no fun at all.

What a dog does *not* need is a once-in-a-while owner — someone who enjoys his dog only when he has no other plans, a day off, and the weather is good. A dog has the same needs each and every day regardless of the weather or his owner's mood. A neglected, bored, under-exercised dog will become a nuisance, eventually becoming a poorly-behaved adult dog who is not welcome anywhere. It should be a pleasure to walk your dog. Then you will do it often and your dog will be well exercised. If it is a dreaded daily chore, requiring a grip of steel and sloppy clothes, your dog will not get walked often enough. He will become chronically under-exercised, bored and eventually figure out destructive ways of getting your attention. Not enough time each day and the dog ends up in the city pound. A little bit of time each day can lead to a great friendship.

No better companion

Whether or not your dog is trained, it is likely that you or someone in your family will grow madly attached to him, preventing you from giving him away no matter how outrageous his behaviour. You will be stuck with him and his habits for ten to fifteen years. Setting rules now will allow you the freedom to take your dog with you almost anywhere and to rely on his good behaviour. You will also be able to leave him alone or with others. When you take him on a walk, he will walk on-leash or off-leash with you in control. Eventually, your roles will switch and he will be watching you, looking out for you at all times. There is no better companion than a well-trained dog.

Deborah's sure-fire basic training strategy

- Always ensure that your dog's basic needs for shelter, food, exercise and mental stimulation are met.
- Always reward good behaviour.
- Never reward bad behaviour (no matter how cute).
- Always redirect bad behaviour to good behaviour, and then praise.
- You can never praise too much in response to good behaviour.
- Spend more time on good behaviour and praise than on bad behaviour and punishment.
- Punish your dog only when you catch him in the act of bad behaviour.
- Giving your dog mixed signals confuses him and sets the stage for failure.
- Clear rules, enforced all the time, make training easy and fun for your dog.
- Dogs like to have a job and to do their job well.
- Use healthy dog foods as training rewards. Use touch and praise as well.
- Make your dog work for every perk, and he'll enjoy the perks more.
- Set the stage for success by controlling your dog to obey commands.

In praise of praise

Praise is your most powerful tool in dog training. If you praise your dog every time she behaves correctly, your dog will become trained in no time. The trick to this training is to stage success and praise. At first, deny your dog the opportunity to defy you by training in an environment where you have total control (for example, your house). You give a command, enforce it and then praise your dog. Eventually, she will respond to the command with an eager attitude because she will want the praise that follows. Then you can extend the setting to more tempting, less controlled situations. Any disobedience and you must revert back to a more controlled set up, and practice until she's back to a 100% correct response. You must be consistent because dogs do not understand "sometimes." Make your rules clear and absolute, and always enforce them.

What about punishment?

Punishment is a dirty word in this book. Most people overuse punishment as a training tool. It should only be used in two situations:

1. Defiant and/or repetitive bad behaviours.
2. "Caught-in-the-act" behaviours.

Punishment must be strict, firm and quick. It must also be followed up by a drill of

Attention! Attention!

If your dog gets more attention for bad behaviour than he does for good, he will learn to behave badly — bad attention is better than no attention at all in your dog's eyes. If it seems like he wants to get caught, like he is stealing things from under your nose and flaunting his bootie, then change your strategy. Ignore the bad behaviour. Let him run around with what he has stolen — he'll get bored when you stop chasing him. Now teach him to do something that you like, and praise him like mad.

commands and praise. This allows your dog to save face and regain your trust. The negative response to negative behaviour should last less than a minute, while the praise-earning commands should last two to four minutes. For example, scold for a "caught-in-the-act" pee in the house, but then immediately direct your dog to her spot outside, encourage her to pee and praise like mad when she does. The message is: peeing in the house = bad; peeing outside = good. Without the second step, your dog will learn only that pee is bad, and try to hold it in at all times or hide it in your home.

Directing your dog through exercises gives her a face-saving alternative to a stand-off with you, and teaches her that proper behaviour earns positive feedback, and that improper behaviour is never tolerated.

Isolation method

This is the most humane and effective method of teaching strict lessons that must be learned. It is especially useful if punishing your dog is distasteful to you, or if your dog is not learning from the domination method.

- Keep a leash on your dog at all times, using it to take him out of the room and into isolation whenever he bites.
- It is important that the place of isolation is not a place he fears or hates. *It is the separation from you and the pack that acts as the punishment, not the place you confine him.* This space must be comfortable and small, such as his kennel.
- Keep his area positive by feeding and praising him there. Also keep special toys there.
- As soon as he bites or nips, catch the leash and scold him with NO BITES as you tug sharply on his neck until he responds. Then march him briskly to the isolation area.
- Leave him there at least twenty minutes, releasing him only when he is calm and quiet. Close the door or cover the kennel with a blanket if necessary to convince him that you will not release him when he cries.
- When he is quiet, take him by the leash and command him to COME. Pull him

towards you, petting and praising with GOOD BOY.

- Now lead him through a series of commands such as SIT, STAY and COME, praising with each good response. If he rebels, scold and march him back to isolation. Repeat the exercise until he understands that he must behave responsively and unaggressively or he will be isolated.

The quick punishment

Hold

Grab your dog in a *pain-free* but completely controlled manner: for small dogs, hold the scruff of his neck with one hand and his stomach with your other; for medium and large dogs, grab hold of both cheeks and hold his head tight; for aggressive dogs, keep him on a trailing leash, then grab the leash tightly.

Look

Stare or glare at your dog with controlled anger as you state your complaint and give your message, such as, NO PEE IN THE HOUSE.

Voice

Give your dog the message in a firm, loud, deep voice, for example, NO BITES.

The quick punishment for a small dog: hold the scruff of his neck with one hand and his stomach with the other.

Consequences for serious or repeat offenses

After reprimanding your dog, march (with or without leash) or carry him in a not-too-com-fortable hold to isolation (his kennel) or, if a pee/poop offense, outdoors. When you are ready to release your dog (after fifteen minutes or so), give him some basic commands and follow with praise.

The quick punishment for a medium- or large-sized dog: tightly hold both cheeks and keep his head high.

The extended praise

After your quick punishment, follow up with a lot of praise. Without it, the punishment will only make your dog avoid you when he knows you're angry. He will still act out, but instead of coming when called, he will dart about just out of reach and never surrender control. Because he will be punished when caught for bad behaviours, he may learn which behaviours provoke you, but he will not learn which behaviours you enjoy. As a result, he will not know how to please you or get your attention in a positive way and will be forced to act out bad behaviours to get noticed.

The quick punishment for an aggressive dog: keep him on a trailing leash (leash attached, but dragging on the ground) so that you can reprimand him quickly. When he misbehaves, grab the leash tightly.

For a positive follow-up to a punishment:

- Run through a quick series of commands that your dog knows well.
- Praise him each time he obeys.

- Make him earn his entry back into the house or from isolation by showing you that he is willing to accept your authority and obey your commands.
- Praise his good behaviour to teach him that your punishment was in reaction to his bad behaviour, and that his good behaviour will produce a good reaction.

A typical face-saving follow-up might sound like this:

- BANDIT, COME, (as he is pulled out of his kennel toward you by leash).
- Touch Bandit, then praise him with, GOOD BOY.
- Enforce a variety of commands:
SIT, enforce, GOOD BOY ... LIE DOWN, enforce, GOOD BOY ... OK, COME, enforce, GOOD BOY ... SIT, enforce, GOOD BOY ... then, once Bandit is responding enthusiastically, release him from the drill with, OK, GOOD BOY.

Dogs aren't humans. They prefer enclosed to open spaces. A kennel creates a den-like, refuge area for Goldie where she:

- Knows what is expected of her.
- Sleeps feeling safe and protected.
- Seeks refuge from pestering children, noises that frighten her or house guests she doesn't like.

Because Goldie is comfortable and happy in her kennel space, you can use it to keep her isolated from you and your family "pack" if she breaks the rules of the pack. Because she will feel secure and comfortable in her kennel, you can use it to prevent her from learning bad habits like chewing, digging and destroying while you are away from home. *Remember — it is the isolation and not the kennel that is the punishment.*

Create a den

Your dog knows instinctively not to foul her den. If she's been cooped up and forced to eat, poop, pee, sleep and live in a small space such as a cage at a pet store, her natural instinct may be temporarily lost, but you can revive it by creating a den in your home.

A kennel makes the best den. It allows a dog a place of her own where she is safe and unbothered by rough children, fireworks or thunderstorms, and gives her a stronger sense of security. Resist the human desire for roominess and choose a kennel only slightly larger than your dog will be at her full-grown size. From a dog's point of view, the cozier, the better. A kennel works better and faster than any other kind of space, and becomes a handy tool in all aspects of training and supervision. In order for a kennel to work, it must be a positive place, one that becomes your dog's beloved personal hang-out. Just like a child's bedroom, this space can be used to isolate your misbehaving dog and provide a positive place to wait out punishment. *Remember: it is separation from you and the pack that is the punishment, not the place you confine him.* To create this kind of environment:

- Choose a command like KENNEL, CAVE, DEN or ROOM as you place her there, praising, cuddling and playing with her.
- At first, try to avoid giving her positive attention outside of the kennel when you are training, so that there is strong incentive for her to obey your command and gain the reward.
- Always insist that your dog obey QUIET as a condition to being released. She must learn that you decide when she can rejoin the pack, and that *crying or carrying on will never lead to release.*

For a kennel alternative, create a confined and cozy space no larger than the appropriate kennel size. Remember, this is not meant to be a play area, but rather a den or sleeping spot.

Meals

Initially, all meals should be fed in the kennel.

1. Command KENNEL, then place some food inside. When trained, you can expect her to enter and sit in response to your command, without the tossed food.

2. Once she enters the kennel, put the dish inside and close the door.

3. Leave her for twenty minutes, then pick up the dish and take her directly outside to her pee and poop spot. Use a leash at first.

4. Always kennel Goldie at night until she is house trained and whenever she is alone until she has gone months without destruction and is over one-and-a half years of age.

5. Sometimes your dog will eat something that upsets her stomach. If she cries uncharacteristically when kenneled, leash and take her to the pee/poop spot. Once she has relieved herself, march her back inside to her kennel.

Kennel tips

- Leave a special chew toy in the kennel at all times.

- Feed meals in the kennel, always at first, then once a day, then once in awhile.

- Throw treats in, and make a game out of the KENNEL command.

- Give the KENNEL command when you feel like cuddling, and cuddle in the kennel.

Whiny dogs & sleepless nights

Goldie will learn the power of her cry if it brings her the result she wants. *Do not release your dog from her kennel because she demands it.* She must learn that barking does not lead to release, but to further isolation (refer to page 68 on QUIET).

In order to rid your dog of this fussy habit:

Proper kennel training will teach your dog that:

• Being kenneled is no big deal and always leads to release.

• Being quiet in her kennel gets her praise, treats, cuddles and freedom.

• Crying gets her nowhere.

• Being alone is no big deal.

1. Start by kenneling her for short periods. For example, when you're watching TV, kennel Goldie for one commercial break. Offer praise and a toy. When the break is over, command her to be QUIET and release her.
2. Let Goldie stay with you until the next break, then put her back in the kennel, again with praise and a toy. This time, leave her longer, keeping her kenneled through the program until the next commercial break. Demand QUIET before release.
3. Repeat this several times, each time kenneling her longer.
4. Any time Goldie gets noisy, separate her from you further by either moving the kennel to another room and shutting the door or throwing a blanket over the kennel. Try both if necessary. No matter what, you must not teach her that making noise will get her released. Be firm now and she'll accept the separation sooner.

Whatever other rules and commands you choose to teach your dog, house training is a must. Be prepared with cleaning products, rags and a mix of equal parts water and vinegar in a spray bottle. Oh — and load up on patience; you're going to need it, especially if you are training an older dog or a pet store survivor.

Step 1: Create a soiling spot in your yard

This should be an area you can see from your home. Mark it by placing small bits of your dog's poop and paper with her urine in the area. A visiting dog using the area will add extra appeal.

Step 2: Establish routine feeding times

Offer breakfast and dinner at the same time each day. This helps your dog with the physical control she needs for house training. Usually, she will want to go out fifteen or twenty minutes after a meal.

Please note: Puppies need to go out immediately after a meal, every two to three hours when awake, every four to six hours if asleep and kenneled and every hour if excited or romping with kids. After ten weeks, most puppies can sleep up to eight hours.

A sample daily routine

Morning:

- Goldie sleeps in her kennel from bedtime till early morning. (She's a young puppy, so she was taken out around midnight for a pee).
- You wake up, take Goldie by leash out of the kennel to outside, say GO PEE several times in an encouraging voice as you march her to her spot. Allow her to sniff around until she pees. Praise her, make a big fuss, then head straight back into the house and put Goldie back in her kennel.
- Goldie eats breakfast in her kennel. After ten or fifteen minutes, march her out to her spot. Again, wait it out no matter how long it takes, and she'll learn fast. If you give up now and bring her back in the house before she poops, training could take weeks.
- Try saying GO POOP while she is doing it, so she will connect the words with the act. Praise her, make a big fuss, then go back inside. Even if you wish to walk, go back inside for a minute or two to keep the pee/poop trip separate from the walk.

Evening:

- Feed Goldie her evening meal in the kennel, then take her out to pee/poop in the same way as after breakfast.

In between meals:

- Chances are Goldie will try to pee or poop inside, because if she does, she feels less full, learns to smell her scent as part of the home territory and becomes convinced that she has chosen an appropriate place to mark. *Do not let her get away with it.* Supervise your dog at all times until she understands the concept and has not made a mistake for several weeks. This means she must always be in your sight, in the same room. When this isn't possible, kennel her until you can supervise her again.

- Every time Goldie comes out of the kennel, she should be marched straight outside to her spot and commanded GO PEE. Wait there until she does, then praise and immediately escort her back inside. Now she is ready to be in the house and free — under your supervision. After an hour or two, if she starts to sniff around or tries to leave you, march her out to her spot and repeat the pee command.

Good dog!

A dog has an almost unlimited ability to pee at any time. Once you give the PEE command, you must wait and not allow her inside until she has peed. As soon as she does, praise her, make a fuss and return directly to the house.

Step 3: Caught in the act

You must never punish your dog for soiling in the house unless you catch her in the act. If you do catch her:

- Grab her quickly in a control hold or snap on a leash.
- Scold her by saying NO PEE IN HOUSE.
- March her outside to her spot and give the command words.
- Wait for her, offering her encouragement and reassurance.
- Praise and fuss when she pees/poops.
- Escort her back inside.

It is very important that your dog be both scolded for soiling in the house, and praised for soiling in her spot. Otherwise, she will learn that all peeing and pooping is bad and will find secretive places to soil. You are showing her first where not to go, and second, where to go. Clean all soiled spots as best you can, then cover liberally with your vinegar-water mix to erase the scent.

Step 4: When your dog starts to catch on

Instead of accompanying your dog outside, stand where you can watch her. Command her to GO PEE as she leaves the house, praising her when she does. Call her to come in once she's done. Do not relax your supervision in the house as this sends mixed signals.

This ain't potty training

Those of you with children know that the best way to teach them to use the toilet is with patience, guidance and praise. The same is true for dogs. There is one major difference, though: dogs are fully capable of understanding and respecting house rules at a very early age.

In nature, their mother teaches them to not soil the den by giving firm reprimands and scolding, and by booting pups out of the den, not allowing them to return until they have soiled outside. If you, as your dog's new parent, allow her to soil the den without redirecting her to soil outside, then she is being taught that soiling inside is acceptable. She must be caught and redirected *every time*. Any mixed messages will confuse her.

Step 5: When your dog is at least one year old and accident-free for two weeks

- Start to leave her unsupervised with her kennel in an extremely small area such as a bathroom.
- Do not close the kennel door.
- If she begins to soil the area, go back to closing the kennel door.
- If she respects the house-training rules, after one week of no mistakes, add another area.
- Allow her one new room each week, supervising her closely when you allow her access to the rooms she most often tried to soil.
- If she has *any* relapses, immediately take her back to the closed-kennel stage and repeat all the house training steps.

Is your best friend ignoring your calls?

Do you stand at the park calling and calling your dog to come — and she doesn't? Do you jump up and down or pretend to drive away, in order to get your wonder pooch to listen — often to no avail? Chances are that somewhere along the line your dog became convinced of one of the following:

COME = "can't catch me" game
COME = punishment
COME = take your time, humans will wait
COME = sometimes humans mean it, sometimes they don't
COME + leash = end of fun

To reverse this thinking, apply the following rules in all situations all the time:

- Always reward or praise your dog when he comes.
- Always enforce COME. If you are too busy or tired, then don't give the command.
- COME must always have the same meaning, that is, COME ALL THE WAY TO ME SO THAT I CAN TOUCH YOU.
- Teach COME when you know your dog will obey — at feeding or walk times.
- Punish him only if you catch him in the act of *not* coming. If he ignores you, get to him before he comes to you, then firmly leash him and practice several times, enforcing and praising each time.

- Stage success by starting in the house. Work up to more tempting situations like the park once your dog is convinced that COME is a good thing.
- Should he at any time relapse and ignore your command, go back to more confined situations. Gradually work up to where he has a great deal of freedom.
- Show strong direction and leadership. Walk away from your dog if he is too slow to obey your command.
- *Never call him with the COME command to punish him. He will think you are punishing him for obeying.*

How to give the COME command

1. Start with your dog on leash. Call him to COME for meals and walks, or from room to room in the house as part of play.
2. Call your dog firmly by name to get his attention: BANDIT!
3. Command him in a firm voice to COME.
4. Say the command word once only. If he disobeys, enforce it immediately by pulling him toward you. Praise when you touch him.
5. Work up to outdoor situations. When your dog is responding reliably on leash, practice with a longer leash, then with the leash trailing, and finally practice COME with no leash at all. After giving the command, show a ball, jog off unpredictably, or hide, to make him see the value in paying attention to COME.
6. Once he COMES, touch him and praise

with GOOD BOY, then release him with new command words: OK, GO. Use food rewards intermittently, gradually fading them out to times of extreme temptation. Substitute with praise and touching.

7. Call your dog several times during the course of a walk. Make sure he stays within a distance you can manage.

Most common COME mistakes

- Hitting or yelling at him when he comes because it took too long. This teaches that COME = punishment.
- Calling several times. This teaches him that ignoring you is okay.
- Calling him when he can't (that is, he doesn't know how to) COME. If you expect too much from an untrained dog, you set the stage for failure.
- Saying COME for many commands. Saying "come closer," "come this way" or "come hurry up" is asking for confusion if what you really mean is "closer," "this way" and "hurry up."
- Changing your mind after saying the command and letting him play longer. He won't listen to you when you do mean it.
- Using COME at the end of walks only. He'll take this to mean COME = end of fun.
- Saying COME and then immediately walking toward your dog as he disobeys you. Your words say COME, but your body says go.
- Allowing kids to call him to play chase games. *COME is a command that must*

maintain its meaning. Teach him other command words for games (for example, PLAY).

- Praising him for an incomplete COME. He will develop "fly by" behaviours and other annoying habits if he is praised for coming near, but not all the way to you.

SIT

Are you being pushed around at mealtimes, forced in and out of doorways or is your white, shedding dog jumping all over your mother's new navy suit? Train your dog to SIT and LIE DOWN and your days of collision and frustration will be over.

Treats are without a doubt the fastest and most effective learning method. Start by letting your dog smell that you have food rewards. Pick a healthy treat and use small amounts. Your dog must learn that the only way to get these rewards is by listening to your commands — no trick = no treat. Hold out on your dog or you will give him mixed signals and confuse him.

Here are two methods to teach SIT:

Off-leash

This is the easiest and preferable method.

1. Stand facing your dog. Hold the treat in a closed fist above and in front of your dog's head.
2. Command him to SIT.
3. Move your hand up and over his head — he will try to keep the treat in focus as you move it behind his eye range and will be naturally inclined to sit.
4. If he jumps up, do not give him the treat. Scold him — NO, OFF — then repeat SIT and the hand motion. Be persistent.

Deborah's Rule of Bum

The only way to earn the treat is to SIT.

Do you mind if I slap your bum?

I've observed that most dogs certainly do. The area immediately before Goldie's tail is an erogenous zone. If you command her to SIT, and then press down on your dog's bum, you are giving mixed messages. When you touch her where she would normally feel the contact of another dog humping her, you are making a pass. If you're her type, Goldie will respond by pressing up and into your hand, opposing your SIT command. If you're not her type, she will respond by trying to avoid your pass and spin her bum out of your reach.

The Off-leash Sit: hold the treat in a closed fit in front of and above the dog's head.

Command her to SIT, while moving your hand with the treat up and over her head.

5. If necessary, place your dog in the SIT position: kneel beside him, than extend your forearm and make contact with both his hind legs just below the knees. Scoop him up and lower him into a SIT position. Then praise.

6. Once he responds reliably to SIT, phase out treats by intermittently substituting praise, touch or a toy. Eventually phase out treat rewards completely.

7. Use mealtimes to make him SIT patiently for his food reward.

On-leash

This method works better for very determined jumpers or for dogs who have learned to ignore SIT.

1. Leash your dog with a short leash and training collar. Loop the handle over your right wrist and grip the leash with your left hand six-to-ten inches from your dog's head (or closer for more control).

2. Walk two to three steps, then stop abruptly with loud foot movements.

3. Command your dog to SIT, pulling up and back on the leash with a short hard tug.

4. Praise him as soon as he sits.

5. If he resists or jumps away, move your left hand closer to his head and continue to give quick hard tugs up and back. Repeat the command word only after he sits, saying SIT, GOOD BOY, as praise.

6. When your dog sits every time, try the off-leash method.

STAY

STAY is an important command for your dog to respect. At home it prevents her from pushing past you to get in or out the door. On walks it helps her to know what is expected of her when she is tied and left to wait for you. STAY can also save your dog from oncoming traffic if she has a tendency to leap out the car door the second it's opened or to run across the street after dogs.

Teach STAY as part of a SIT and STAY drill. Stand with your dog at your left side. Command her to SIT, praising her.

SIT ... GOOD DOG ... STAY.

- Turn to face her. Then, with your flat hand held in front of her face, palm forward, command her to STAY.
- If she moves, gently place her back in the SIT and remind her to STAY at first.

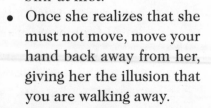

- Once she realizes that she must not move, move your hand back away from her, giving her the illusion that you are walking away.
- If she stays, wait for two seconds, then move your hand back toward her and step back to her side. *Praise her as you touch her, and release her with OK.*
- Repeat this exercise until you are able to make her stay for five seconds, giving the command only once.

SIT ... GOOD DOG ... STAY.

Once your dog has learned to SIT reliably off-leash, it is time to teach him an extension of the sit — to LIE DOWN.

1. Using the off-leash method, command your dog to SIT.
2. If he responds properly, reward him with half a treat and praise.
3. Hold the remaining half-treat with a closed fist in the same start position as you did for the SIT command, above and in front of his eyes.
4. Command him to LIE DOWN, as you drop your closed fist down to the floor in front of him, just below his head and in front of his paws.
5. He will be naturally inclined to follow the treat with his nose and drop to his tummy.
6. Praise and reward him with the treat.

If your dog resists, jumps about or digs at your hands, refusing to pay attention to the LIE DOWN command, then you need to exert more control. Practice these on-leash exercises:

More control

1. Leash your dog with a short leash held close to his head in your left hand.
2. Enforce the on-leash SIT command and reward him with praise.
3. Turn to face your dog. Give the LIE DOWN

command as you pull the leash down-ward, forcing your dog's neck to the ground.

4. Praise and touch him in the LIE DOWN position. Give him a treat when he stops resisting.

5. Repeat until perfect.

6. Teach him to obey LIE DOWN using the off-leash method.

Do you walk your dog, or does your dog walk you? Believe it or not, *your* dog can and should learn to walk respectfully by your side, making sure not to pull or cause you to trip for any reason.

Equipment you'll need

- Choke collar suitable for your dog's neck size and fur type.

or

- Gentle Leader or Promise collar for more severe leash-pullers.
- A short (no longer than four to six feet), non-extending leash made of material that has a comfortable handle.

If the collar fits...

Puppies grow quickly, and dogs can put on weight. Collars can be outgrown rapidly, so check regularly for the proper fit of your dog's collar. A too-tight collar can choke your dog, or cause painful wounds.

Stick to the rules

For training to work quickly, you must enforce the rules during walks with no exceptions. This is not cruel: acting lenient or relaxed even once in a while will confuse your dog, who will not understand what is expected of him.

Rule 1: Only use the HEEL command when a strict HEEL is expected.

Rule 2: Walk briskly as you give the HEEL command.

Rule 3: Never allow your dog to drag, trip or otherwise disrespect you.

GOOD DOG!

Choke collar

A choke collar is only effective if it is placed properly on your dog's neck. Otherwise, it causes pain and does not work as a training aid. Make sure the collar slides easily without catching on your dog's fur and is long enough to allow for two to three inches of slack. It is essential to correct your dog with quick short tugs, because the collar must tighten and release to give him the proper message. If you are using the choke collar properly, it will make a jingling sound each time you tug and release. Don't "water-ski" behind your "motorboat" dog (holding on tight, with no control, at the very end of the leash); this is cruel as it causes constant pressure on the dog's throat. To avoid choking, hold the leash closer to your dog's head and give corrections with strong, upward, jerking motions.

Rule 4: Always praise nice walking.

Rule 5: Demand and enforce a strict heel once you say HEEL.

Rule 6: Use a different command like WALK or WALK NICELY for a less strict walk.

Walk the heel walk

- Slip the handle over your right wrist and firmly grip the leash with your left hand, approximately half-an-arm's length from your dog's head (closer for more control and less muscle strain).

- Your left hand is the Control Hand. Use your grip to correct your dog's position with short, quick tugs on the leash. Tug in an up and back motion at a 45-degree angle from the dog's head, and then immediately release.

- The tug and release *must* be immediate. If constant pressure is maintained, your dog will be choking, not learning.

- Begin your walk with the HEEL command.

- Place your dog with tugs on the leash into the proper position by your left knee.

- When he heels, praise with GOOD BOY.

- Repeat this pattern. All your dog should hear during this training walk is the command and praise words: HEEL ... tug ... GOOD DOG. This will teach him that by walking in position he avoids neck tugging and earns praise.

- Once he has mastered the regular step, vary your pace (for example, walk ten steps, then jog, then run like mad), change direction unpredictably or do figure eights. Your dog will listen to your foot steps, so stamp your feet for emphasis when you change your walk. Challenge your dog to play along and match your steps in HEEL.

If your dog is a determined puller ...

You must teach your dog that pulling will not get him where he wants to go. Start in situations where he is less tempted to pull and work up to hard ones such as park entrances and fire hydrants. Prepare for a struggle the first few times and stay firm. The struggle will soon end, and you will have won your dog's respect.

When walking with a determined puller ...

- Use a Promise collar or a Gentle Leader to give you full control at all times, and to avoid excessive neck-tugging.
- Always insist that your dog approach the

Promise or Gentle Leader

These are trade names of two very effective and by far the most humane training collars. They cause no pain and are simple to use. They look like a muzzle, so many people think they are cruel. They're not. They give complete control over your dog's head with only a slight pull. The pressure on a dog's nose causes no discomfort, cannot choke the dog, and allows him to move more naturally. And since pressure over the bridge of the nose is a signal of dominance, these collars are effective with dominant dogs and can help to curb aggression. A small child can walk a large dog using a Promise Collar once both are properly trained. The key to training with this collar is the first session. The dog must not be allowed to try to remove the collar. Keep it attached to the leash, hold the leash with your left hand gripped close to the dog's head and jerk sharply if the dog tries to remove the collar with his paw or by rolling on the ground. Walk and tug him as you command HEEL. Use this collar for all leash walks so that he will associate it with walks and so that you will be consistent with your HEEL training.

object of his desire at a respectful HEEL walk.

- When he pulls, pivot and turn your body as you force him to HEEL to your steps with quick firm tugs.
- Each time he starts to pull, turn him away from the object, turning back towards it only when he's calm. Don't be afraid to make him circle back five or ten times.
- Your dog will soon learn that he will get close to the object when he HEELS, and that pulling toward an object will only get him further away.

Walking in circles

For dogs that pull throughout the walk, start with a very strict HEEL drill. March in a large circle, and begin the walk only when he is heeling properly. If he pulls during the walk, return to the circle drill until he responds.

Shock collar, prong collar or any collar designed to inflict pain

I strongly discourage the use of these collars. They are cruel and the results are always an unpredictable dog.

Flat-buckle collar

Use this collar for everyday use when not in training.

Leashes

Use a four to six-foot leash made of material that is comfortable to hold. Avoid retractable and elasticized leashes.

Shopping tip

Bring your dog with you when purchasing training equipment and ask the salespeople to show you how to fit and use products correctly.

The easiest time to teach your dog to stay with you off-leash is when she's under five months. Young pups are afraid of new people and noises and find comfort in walking at your side. Having said this, it is never too late to teach the WITH ME command. When your dog will COME and HEEL reliably, you are ready to begin.

Start the session

- HEEL walk your dog with a leash and training collar to a safe, off-leash area.
- Allow some off-leash play, practicing and enforcing COME. Up the incentive with treats or toys.
- Once she is no longer raring to go and darting in all directions, leash her, and with a strict HEEL, leave the park area.

Ready

- Walk a block or two until she knows she is not in the park with its freedoms.
- Select a safe area to work off-leash.
- If your dog is responsive and not likely to bolt, try this with no leash at all. If your dog loves to run and seems oblivious to you, keep the leash on, allowing it to trail. This gives you a psychological edge, and will allow you to take control more easily. If your dog is famous for taking off, attach an extra long leash, a rope, or two or three leashes strung together.

Leash range

For beginners, it is easiest if you establish a circular range of five to ten feet with you at the centre. Stick with it, recalling your dog each time he strays out of the imaginary circle. One he has fully understood WITH ME for one month, you may start to vary the range from walk to walk. Always set the range at the start of each walk.

With me

- Once your dog is happily adhering to HEEL, release her with an OK, WITH ME.

- As you say this, let go of the leash (or remove it) and tap your side. This shows her that this is not an OK, GO situation, but a new command.

- Make yourself interesting by carrying balls or treats, and walk briskly. If she strays too far, call her by name, then remind her WITH ME as you slap your side for emphasis.

- Show a treat or toy to entice her closer.

- She should respond by moving closer. Give her the treat or ball and praise her when she does, then re-establish the WITH ME command as you set off at a brisk pace once again.

- Try to be consistent, recalling her when she strays from you each and every time.

- Establish a stray zone and stick to it. I recommend a five-foot zone for beginners and a ten-foot zone when she is more advanced.

- Once she has learned to stay close and keep up with you, make WITH ME more fun: act unpredictably, turn suddenly, speed up or slow down to make a game out of this command. This is especially helpful for smart, hyper dogs like Border Collies who crave challenges. You'll know if your dog fits into this category!

When your dog is behaving, the commands sound like this:

WITH ME ... she gets closer ... GOOD GIRL ... start walking ... WITH ME.

Practice makes perfect

- After a few minutes, leash and HEEL walk your dog again for equal time.
- Then repeat the WITH ME walk.
- When your dog consistently understands and obeys WITH ME in non-tempting situations, you will be ready to work up to tempting locations like park entrances and places with ducks.

Non-responsive dogs

- Try to enforce the command by stepping on her trailing leash and scolding her: NO, I SAID WITH ME.
- Pull her towards you, saying WITH ME, and praise her for respecting the command.
- Continue walking. If she tries to bolt, give her the HEEL command, and enforce it until she is paying close attention and listening well. Repeat the exercise by letting the leash trail again.
- If this method does not give you enough control, try walking her on-leash, but teaching her that even with a long leash, she must stay close and allow for slack. Eventually, you can work up to having the leash trail and finally, no leash at all. Move up a level only when she is consistently responding to the command. Be prepared to move back again whenever she tests you and disobeys.

ROAD COMMANDS

All dogs, no matter how well trained, are at risk when off-leash near roads. Road commands are designed to make your dog aware of the distinction between streets and safe areas such as sidewalks, parks and yards. The command words will teach her specific behaviours. These commands should be practiced and reinforced while on all walks, and should help to get her to respond in off-leash emergencies.

On-leash

Every time you step out onto a street or laneway, no matter how small or quiet, you must show your dog that there is an important distinction to be made between off-road and road.

SIT ... GOOD DOG.

WAIT.

1. Stop at the curbside of a street.
2. Command your dog to SIT. The walk must not continue under any circumstances until she obeys. Praise her when she does.
3. Command her to WAIT. Stand perfectly still, controlling her on a short leash, and hold your hand palm open facing her.
4. Instruct her to OK, CROSS only when she is respecting your SIT-WAIT.
5. Step out and onto the street. Keep her on a very short leash to enforce a HEEL as you briskly walk her across the street.
6. Say OFF ROAD when you near the opposite side.
7. Praise her once her feet hit the non-road surface.

Once your dog patiently and obediently obeys your road commands, you may scale

OK, CROSS..

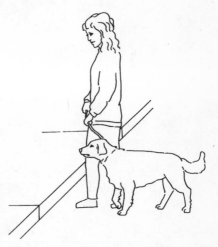

OFF ROAD ... GOOD DOG.

down and omit the SIT. But she must always WAIT and only cross the street when you command CROSS. If she ever relapses, go back to her original training.

In emergencies, should you see your dog about to step onto a street, stop her with WAIT. If you catch her when she's already stepped onto the road, command her to get OFF ROAD.

Advanced road commands

Once Bandit has learned to SIT at all road crossings and obey your road commands, teach him to SIT and WAIT through distractions. He must learn that, even if you step out onto the road or if someone else calls to him, he must not cross until you have given the specific command words OK, CROSS.

DOWN or OFF

In this world, there are two kinds of people: those who like dogs and those who don't. You can bet that for most of the latter group, this lifelong dislike began when a dog jumped on them. Who can blame them? Jumping on people is not nice. There are plenty of other ways for your dog to show excitement and friendliness without barging into a human's personal space. Here's how to teach him how to win friends and influence people:

- Leash your dog.
- Have a favourite person approach.
- Snap the leash to keep him down as you instruct DOWN or OFF.
- Praise him once he is truly not trying to jump at all.

If your dog insists on jumping, ask the person to step away. Allow your dog to figure out that he will only get to greet his friend with four on the floor. When he obeys your DOWN, have the person approach and pet him. Keep the leash by the door or on your dog so you can gain control when visitors come over.

Stubborn jumpers

If he obeys your DOWN command but immediately jumps up, or ignores your command completely, teach him to SIT for all greetings instead. Enforce DOWN or SIT on walks as you pass people or whenever he acts out and jumps up.

DOWN nevers

- Never allow anyone to cuddle, praise or feed your dog when he jumps on them.

- Never allow kids to encourage jumping up as part of play.

Down down down

It is important that your dog understand several words — such as DOWN or OFF — for the DOWN command since the stranger he is greeting may not know which word you've taught him.

QUIET

Does your dog bark out orders? Do not obey him. If you give your dog attention, food or praise in response to barking, you create a demanding pet. Avoid situations where you are forced to give in to prevent embarrassing scenes or hassles with neighbours. Make sure that barking for attention always leads to a bad result for your dog, not you.

Start work on QUIET early and, as always, be consistent.

- When you kennel your dog, insist on QUIET after a few seconds. Praise him if he obeys.
- Release him from the kennel only when he is quiet, never when he is crying or whining.
- If he protests with noise, scold him and remind him to be QUIET. Be careful about giving him too much attention.
- If he persists, leave him. Start by leaving the room. If more emphasis is needed, close the room door or cover the kennel with a towel or blanket, or do both. If his cries are too compelling for you to withstand, leave the house or turn up the TV or stereo.

Once your dog is responding to QUIET in the kennel, extend his learning to play.

- If he barks playing FETCH (see page 121), command him with QUIET and throw the ball only when he is quiet.

- Should he bark incessantly, demanding the ball be thrown, end the game by putting the ball away. Again, you are teaching him that barking ends the game and that QUIET leads to play.

Noisy dogs and determined barkers

- Keep a leash on your dog at all times. When you remind him to be QUIET, grab the leash and jerk sharply to emphasize your command.
- Tug and release the leash several times if necessary, denying him freedom in order to enforce QUIET.
- When he has learned QUIET, you should gradually allow him more freedom, first by loosening your hold on the leash, later by letting the leash trail. Be prepared to step on or grab the leash should he start barking again.
- A Gentle Leader or Promise Collar will help a great deal with a noisy dog.

Bark on command

After your dog is responding to QUIET and respecting the QUIET rules of play, you may want to teach him to bark, or SPEAK, on command. A sweetheart dog that will bark in response to your command can seem like a guard dog and will intimidate unwanted strangers or intruders. Always practice QUIET at least once every time you encourage him to SPEAK.

GOOD DOG!

Avoid arguments

If your dog barks back at you when you command QUIET, do not make the QUIET command louder and sharper. This only encourages him to bark. When you say the word QUIET say it firmly, but say it slowly, imitating the response you wish. Sound calm and firm like a school librarian, not loud and aggressive. If your dog wants to argue, leash him and control him. If he seems determined to have the last word, kennel him.

- Command SPEAK, imitating his bark with the word. Bark at him and encourage him when he barks.
- Repeat the command and praise him: SPEAK, GOOD BOY.
- Next, remind him to be QUIET, giving him a treat as you do so. Since he cannot eat and bark at the same time, he will be quiet to eat the treat. Praise him as he does so.
- Make the reward for QUIET greater than the reward for speak by giving food or toys only to reward the QUIET.
- Take advantage of times when he is barking appropriately to command him to SPEAK.
- Praise him afterwards.

HAND SIGNALS

When your dog has mastered the basic commands, it is time to teach him to respond to hand signals also. Start with the command he knows best, and emphasize the hand signal as you say the command word. At first, get your dog's attention by whistling, then say the word as you normally do while you make the hand signal. Review three or four times, then repeat with just the hand signal. Whenever he ignores your hand signal, enforce the command as you repeat the signal and say the word.

Author's note:

This chapter is a general look at this problem and is not a substitute for the help and advice of a professional trainer or a veterinarian with behavioural training experience.

It's one thing to have a guard dog, well-trained to react to specific situations. It's quite another to have a dog who attacks or bites unprovoked. You want your dog to be confident and well-adjusted, socialized to interact with people and other dogs and to deal with a variety of situations. A dog who becomes anxious when left alone, is under-exposed to different experiences, is over-coddled and protected, or is neglected and subjected to painful punishment, becomes a danger. He may look tough, but he's terrified, unreliable and likely to make poor judgement calls.

How do you know if your dog is afraid or aggressive? Check out the next section on Body Posture, and ask yourself these questions:

1. Does your dog tremble, urinate, roll over or run and hide when new people come over?
2. Does your dog whine and yelp when left alone?
3. Does your dog claw and chew at himself or his kennel when left alone?

4. Does your dog cower when new dogs approach, no matter how inoffensive they may be? Does he stand perfectly still with his eyes averted or growl unprovoked?
5. Does your dog squeal or make a big fuss about minor grooming or health care procedures like nail clipping?
6. Does your dog fly off the handle with visitors, working himself into a barking frenzy?
7. Does your dog bark incessantly at almost everything and everyone, no matter how familiar?
8. Does your dog bark or growl and charge dogs or people who approach when he's off-leash?
9. Does your dog strain on the leash, lunging in the direction of other dogs as he growls and snarls challenges?

And last, but most important:

10. DOES YOUR DOG BITE?

If you had to answer yes to *any* of these questions, you have a dog with fears that could lead to aggression. Consult "Nipping & Biting" on page 93 for specifics on bite inhibition, and "Praise & Punishment" on page 25 for the "how-to" of discipline.

Sometimes behavioural problems have a physiological cause. If your dog has chronic behaviour problems, always consult your vet before taking a behavioural approach.

Create security

Reliable routines help to alleviate the insecurity and anxiety that come from basic fears such as starvation, pain, abandonment, neglect and the threat from tougher dogs.

Feeding times

Give your dog two meals a day at the same time mornings and evenings. Put the food down inside his kennel or den, close him in there with no other pets and leave him for twenty minutes. Remove the food whether he's eaten or not and do not feed him again until the next mealtime.

Walk times and sleep times

Establish the same times each day.

Get rid of aggression: the strategy

- *Always* interfere with your dog's aggressive behaviours.
- Re-direct aggressive behaviour in a controlled manner to positive behaviour such as HEEL.
- Praise new good behaviours.
- Control through easy situations and work up to more challenging ones.

Start by building confidence

- Handle your dog often. If he is fighting you, tie and/or muzzle him at first to

Touch

Within a pack setting, touch is far more important than words. As a result, your dog is more receptive to information through touch. For an ego boost or an ego check, let your fingers do the walking:

Confidence building

When you pet and stroke your dog's chin and chest while he sits or stands, you are touching him as a young pup or a submissive dog would. This will confirm his higher and taller status, and promote calm and confidence.

Ego check

When you pet and touch the top of your dog's head or the bridge of his nose, you are touching him the way a pack leader would, confirming his lower and submissive status. This will keep him feeling smaller than you, and may be helpful with a dominant or aggressive dog.

eliminate the struggle. Touch him gently and calmly, praising him as you go. Make sure to handle his paws, mouth, rear, tail and head every day. Cuddle him in a belly-up position.

- Use control and praise to guide your dog to behave nicely and to heel properly when on-leash.
- Force him to experience new situations and dogs with his new behaviour. This convinces him that these experiences can be peaceful and successful.
- Do not chase away dogs Bandit has provoked. He will think you want him to keep other dogs away.
- Do not rescue Bandit from larger dogs. This teaches him that he needs rescuing.

Aggression with humans

Once again, this is a general look at a potentially very serious problem. *Do not hesitate to seek advice from a trainer or veterinarian if you think that any person or other pet is in danger*. At the very least, you should use a Promise collar on all walks for at least one month before exposing a very aggressive dog to strangers. Only introduce new circumstances when he has fully accepted the collar and your control.

Your dog has a natural instinct to protect himself and the members of his pack from non-pack strangers. You must teach him that strangers are a part of regular life and must be treated non-aggressively when they are no threat. If your dog accepts your decisions on other issues and obeys your commands, training him to be friendly will be easy. If, however, your dog challenges your authority on many issues, and often disobeys you, then this issue is going to be tough and should be approached once you have gained control in the basic command areas.

If your dog bites a member of your family or pack, I strongly suggest that you seek the advice of a professional trainer. Techniques similar to those described in "Nipping & Biting" and in the earlier part of this chapter can be used to teach a dog that if he is aggressive with a family member he gets scolded and kenneled. When he behaves he gets freedom, socialization and treats. The trick to this training is to deny the dog the things he loves when he behaves aggressively. You must kennel him every time he is mean — with no exceptions — if you want him to learn that biting humans is always forbidden.

Curbing aggression

- Teach your dog to HEEL. Not just any old heel, but a completely controlled, strict, military-style HEEL. Practice on every walk, every day. Use a different command like WALK or WALK NICELY for a less strict walk. Once your dog has learned to respond 100% and walks obediently next to your left leg, *behind* your knee, you are ready to take him near strangers.

- Visit an area where human traffic is light. Allow him the relaxed leash walk, every so often enforcing a strict HEEL for ten to twenty paces, then releasing him with OK, WALK NICELY. Praise him often.

Give an inch…

There can only be one leader on the walk. If Bandit walks behind your knee, the leader is you. If he pushes forward, you become the follower. Give him an inch and he'll pull you for a mile.

GOOD DOG!

There are no bad dogs

Rotweilers, German shepherds and other dogs with a bad rap can be wonderfully gentle and kindhearted. If you raise a dog properly, no matter what breed or breeds, he can be a gentle, well-behaved dog.

Are some breeds more aggressive than others? You bet, and that means that teaching gentleness is harder work with some than with others. Any breed designed for fighting will give you a challenge in terms of manners around other dogs. Common fighting dogs include the shar pei, chow chow, pit bull terrier and akita. Most terriers need hard work to get then socialized to other animals.

As for the guard dog types, I believe that, when raised properly, these dogs are the most reliable and least likely to make bad judgement calls since they are big and tough and have nothing to fear.

- When he is listening well, approach strangers or allow them to approach and pass you. Do not stop, visit, or talk to them. Just walk by. At first, keep a good distance between you and them as you pass each other. Later, allow strangers to pass at a closer distance.
- Maintain control with a tight leash held close to the head, and quick jerks upward on the leash. Walk briskly and command HEEL as you pass the stranger. Praise your dog. If he tries to attack, walk briskly away and tug him several times, reminding him to HEEL. Praise only when he obeys your command.
- Start slow, with people in the distance, and work up to the more scary situations like a fast-moving pack of male joggers, cyclists, or a group of kids.

After you have made serious progress and your dog is now heeling every time you pass strangers, you are ready for the next phase.

- HEEL walk your dog by a stranger or two, and praise him for his good behaviour.
- When you pass the kind of person your dog most enjoys, allow him a little more slack as you pass. Keep your hand on the leash and be ready to tug should he lunge or growl.
- Instruct him to BE NICE and allow him a second or two to sniff the stranger.
- Praise him if he's calm, then command HEEL and tug him as you walk briskly away. Praise him again.

- If he reacts badly, scold him as you pull him back and enforce a strict HEEL. Go back to the earlier exercises and try again at a later date.
- Try to control your dog so that he has no choice but to either BE NICE or be made to HEEL, with no attacks possible. Teach him that if he behaves nicely or heels properly, he gets praise and freedom, and that if he behaves aggressively, he gets scolded and controlled.

Aggression essentials

- Make your dog earn every privilege and perk.
- Cut out all free attention and treats.
- Keep a leash on him at all times, and grab it when you anticipate trouble.
- When he acts out, take control by stepping on the leash or grabbing it, then scold him with NO BITES.
- Remind him of the instruction BE NICE, then yank him back on the leash and escort him to his kennel if he is still wild.
- If your dog calms down, praise him and allow him to stay with you.
- If he still acts aggressively, kennel him.

Eventually, your dog will calm down when you jerk him back and give the BE NICE command. If you enforce the rules consistently, he will learn BE NICE in no time and will be a more relaxed and happy dog as a result. If you enforce the rules only some of the time, he will think his aggressive

Dogs are sexist

Both male and female dogs have a great deal more tolerance with dogs of the opposite sex than with dogs of their own. This is because within a large pack, there are two completely separate pecking orders with an alpha male leader and an alpha female leader. The two alphas would be mates and equals within separate spheres of authority determined by their skills and personalities. Within the pack, there is rarely a need for a male and female to fight one another. This means that it will be much easier to socialize your dog with dogs of the oppostie gender before you begin work on dogs of the same gender.

behaviour is appropriate since it is allowed sometimes, and will not understand why he is punished the rest of the time.

Aggression with other dogs

If Bandit scraps with other dogs, take him to an off-leash park where other dogs run free:

Muzzle tough

Muzzles make a dog feel vulnerable and defenseless, and will not help to teach him confidence. If you need more control, use a Gentle Leader or Promise collar. Familiarize him with it by using it on all walks for two weeks.

- Keep Bandit on leash, holding it firmly and close to his head.
- Every time he exhibits any aggression, jerk quickly and firmly on the leash, several times if necessary, as you command him to HEEL.
- Keep walking no matter what. This shows strong leadership.
- When he accepts your re-direction and HEELS, praise him.
- At first, start your walk far from the other dogs, but as he behaves better, move closer. Finally march him right by them and demand that he HEEL.
- When Bandit automatically and willingly HEELS as you pass new dogs, begin to slow your pace.
- Eventually, allow him a sniff or two. If he freezes or acts aggressively, tug sharply and resume your HEEL walk. Try a visit again soon, if possible with the same dog.
- Once Bandit behaves consistently well, start increasing the sniff time to a visit. If he reverts to aggressive behaviour, scale back to a HEEL walk.

Fearful greeters

If Bandit rolls over and piddles on the floor every time you greet him, he is not trying to anger you. He is submitting to you. Yelling, scolding or punishing will only make him submit more. To end this:

- Hold Bandit so that he is forced to greet you in a SIT position.
- Tell him to SIT and praise him, even if he is trying to lie down or is still piddling.
- Encourage Bandit to SIT and praise him every time you greet him.
- When others come over, keep Bandit on-leash and force him to keep his SIT position by holding the leash tight so that he cannot lie down or roll over.
- Praise him for sitting. Eventually he will figure out that you like to be greeted by a SIT, not a piddle.

More confidence building

To deal with submission problems more generally, you must help your dog to gain confidence. Introduce your dog to new situations and familiarize him with new settings. Teach him tricks so that he can earn praise and gain self-esteem.

Loud greeters

- Keep Bandit on-leash. If he is barking or whining, grab the leash close to his head and tug sharply, commanding QUIET. If he responds, praise him. If he continues to bark, give him three commands he knows, such as SIT, STAY and COME, or SIT, SHAKE PAW and LIE DOWN.
- Enforce and praise. Demand QUIET. If he continues to bark, kennel him.
- If you are arriving home, command Bandit to SIT and be QUIET before opening the door to his room. If he starts to bark,

shut the door, then repeat and enforce your commands. When Bandit is quiet, praise him and allow him to greet you.

Lunging greeters

- Allow your dog no off-leash freedom until he earns it.
- Take Bandit on a short, then long leash, to places with people and dogs. Use the leash to prevent him from lunging at people. Enforce DOWN or OFF, and HEEL.
- Teach him to come and heel in these situations. When he is 100% reliable, take him to a low-traffic area and start off-leash work with the leash trailing (so that you can grab it, if necessary).
- When he reverts to lunging, step on the leash, scolding briefly as you yank him down and command DOWN or OFF.
- Praise him, command COME, pull him closer and praise, then command HEEL, start walking, tug him into position and praise. The command sequence should go something like this:
  BANDIT, DOWN ... yank ... GOOD BOY
  COME ... pull and touch ... GOOD BOY
  HEEL ... tug and walk ... GOOD BOY
- Ask people to pet him only when he SITS.

Body Language

Dogs communicate with each other through body posture. The following illustrations indicate the emotion or message being expressed by a particular stance or gesture.

Massage your dog

It may sound flaky, but massage is the closest our human hands can come to the healing, stroking tongue of the other dogs who would care for your dog in a pack. Cup your hand loosely and start by massaging in counter-clockwise circles gently and slowly. When your dog presses into your hand, increase the pressure; when he moves away, be more gentle. Focus on massaging the chest, chin and mouth of fearful dogs to help them gain more confidence.

Ears back, tail erect, teeth showing, standing as tall as possible.

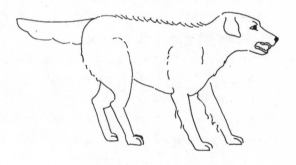

Hunkered down, fur up on back, snarling, ears forward, back straight.

When cornered — head up, mouth open, ears stiff and back.

FEAR

Stone straight, hair up, tail straight out.

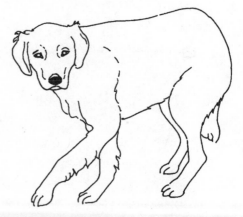

Making himself as small as possible.

Running away with tail between legs, rear tucked underneath.

DOMINATION

Two dogs side by side, one trying to get head over other's neck and back.

Two dogs of same gender humping.

Two dogs, one placing head over other's muzzle and snarling.

Two-dog face-off with posturing and facial expressions.

Licking muzzle of another dog from underneath.

Cowering, tail and ears tucked, low to the ground, piddling.

Rolling over, belly up.

Front down, rear up, tail wagging.

Straight back, legs extended, head up and in wolf-call position, usually talking.

Your pup has a natural urge to nip and bite. In nature his mom taught him when and what not to bite. You must teach your dog that, in your pack, biting humans is never acceptable.

To do this, you must first control how you play with your dog. Start by eliminating all games with play-biting or nipping and tug-of-war. Also eliminate toys that are similar to off-limits possessions of yours. The difference between an old shoe and a brand new one is too subtle for dogs. Interfere when your dog bites or nips anybody. Be vigilant, allowing no exceptions.

Potential trouble areas

- Rough play or play-fighting. This leads to confusion and accidents.
- Tug-of-war. This is an aggressive battle over possession.
- Meals. Kennel or isolate your dog at human mealtimes to avoid meal sharing.
- Children. Large groups should be avoided until the dog is experienced with kids.
- Incorrect disciplining. This can cause the dog to be aggressive and/or to learn to ignore command words.

There are two attitudes that go with biting behaviours. Choose the method of training determined by your dog's attitude.

Group 1: Don't-know-better biters

This group includes all pups four months or under, and dogs who have been untrained or mistrained. These dogs will stop biting when you react negatively, but may go back to it seconds later. They stop because they sense your disapproval, but start to bite again because they have not connected your disapproval with biting.

To train them out of it:

1. When your dog bites or nips you or an object he is not allowed, firmly scold him, saying NO BITES as you open his mouth and remove it from your clothing or body.
2. Immediately place a toy in his mouth, commanding him to GET YOUR TOY, praising him as you hold the toy, allowing him to chew.
3. When he drops the toy and tries for you or your clothing once again, repeat the process, this time a little more firmly.
4. If he still persists in nipping or biting, then kennel him away from you and the other family pack members. Teach him that if he insists on biting, no one wants to be with him.
5. Once your dog has learned to bite and chew *only* his toys, he may still nip as part of play. Instruct him to BE GENTLE as you grab him by his collar. If he fights, kennel him. If he accepts, praise him for his gentle behaviour.

6. Eventually you will only need to remind him to BE GENTLE occasionally.

Group 2: Defiant biters

You probably know if you've got a defiant biter. These dogs demand attention, and will use their teeth to get it. They nip in play, getting rougher and rougher when ignored. They also bite if forced to obey a command they have ignored or resisted. Sometimes these dogs will bite to keep their favourite place on the bed or fight a human for food.

If your dog is bossing you around, teach him that you always get your way. Whenever he exhibits a snarl, raised lip, growl or if he snaps at you, react immediately and completely.

There are two ways to approach this problem — isolation or domination. The choice depends on your comfort level with your dog.

Too tense

Dogs who bite hold a lot of tension in the neck, jaw and mouth. When you are getting along well and both of you are relaxed, touch him in the areas he most likes and gradually work up to making very light, small circles around his nose and mouth. Make sure you provide good, challenging chew toys that your dog likes.

It is extremely important for all training exercises that you teach your dog to tolerate and enjoy your touch and praise.

Isolation method

This is the most humane and effective method of teaching strict lessons that must be learned. It is especially useful if dominating your dog is distasteful to you, or if your dog is not learning from the domination method.

- Keep a leash on your dog at all times, using it to take him out of the room and into isolation whenever he bites.
- It is important that the place of isolation

is not a place he fears or hates. *It is the separation from you and the pack that acts as the punishment, not the place you confine him.* This space must be comfortable and small, such as his kennel.

- Keep his area positive by feeding and praising him there. Also keep special toys there.

- As soon as he bites or nips, catch the leash and scold him with NO BITES as you tug sharply on his neck until he responds. Then march him briskly to the isolation area.

- Leave him there at least twenty minutes, releasing him only when he is calm and quiet. Close the door or cover the kennel with a blanket if necessary to convince him that you will not release him when he cries.

- When he is quiet, take him by the leash and command him to COME. Pull him towards you, petting and praising with GOOD BOY.

- Now lead him through a series of commands such as SIT, STAY and COME, praising with each good response. If he rebels, scold and march him back to isolation. Repeat the exercise until he understands that he must behave responsively and unaggressively or he will be isolated.

Domination method

Please note: Use this method only two or three times for each offense. If your dog continues to fight you, switch to the isolation method. Do not try this method at all if you are afraid your dog might seriously harm you.

While I prefer the isolation method in almost all cases, some traditional dog training methods advocate domination holds. If the isolation method does not appeal to you, try these holds. *Please* — do not cause pain.

Small dogs

Pick him up, making sure not to cuddle him. Grab him by the scruff of the neck with one hand, supporting his belly with the other, as you hold him in the air facing you. Flip him over in your arms into a position of submission.

Medium dogs

Push him to the ground and hold him still, belly up.

Large dogs

Attach a leash to a control collar and leave it on the dog permanently until his aggression is handled. A Promise Collar is best for this training. Grab the leash close to his head when you need to assert yourself, and with

Go to your room

For the best results, practice domination exercises in calm, *non-conflict* situations to most effectively teach your dog that you are *always* in charge.

Do not dominate your dog in front of your kids since they may copy you incorrectly, mess up your training, and possibly get bitten. In a bustling family household, the isolation method works much better. The kids have their bedrooms, the dog has his kennel.

a series of quick upward tugs, gain control and hold him still

Once your dog is in a hold, stare him in the face. *Be careful.* This is a domination posture. An aggressive dog may react strongly. Let your anger come through your words as you demand NO BITES.

All dogs

When your dog relaxes or submits, command BE GENTLE, allowing him to lick your hand and sit up.

Immediately give him a series of commands. Show him that you are boss. Try commands he knows well, like SIT, STAY and COME. Enforce each command and then praise. The punishment should last only a few seconds, while the commands and praise can last up to several minutes.

Directing your dog through positive exercises gives him a face-saving alternative to a standoff with you and teaches him that good behaviour gets good feedback, while nipping and biting is never tolerated.

Whether your dog is tolerant of children depends on his breed and personality. But any dog, no matter how sweet-tempered, can be pushed beyond his limits by poorly behaved children. *Dogs and kids should be supervised at all times.*

It is up to the adult to establish the rules. Children must be taught how to touch and play with a dog, and prevented from ever frightening or harming one:

- Use a leash in the beginning to ensure total control. Keep a Promise Collar on at all times until aggression is reduced.
- Have the children lead the dog through simple tricks, mimicking your training words and giving the dog praise or treats each time he obeys them.
- If the dog acts aggressively towards the children, yank sharply on the leash several times and scold with NO BITES.
- If he responds, then instruct with BE NICE and praise him. If he does not respond, isolate him as described above. *Do not use the domination method — your kids might copy and try to dominate or scold your dog unsupervised.*

Dogs nip kids for lots of reasons. Here are some of the most common:

- Dog is afraid or pestered.

- Dog is hurt or cornered.

- Dog is excited into a frenzy.

- Dog loves kids and considers them his littermates.

- Dog is jealous of kids and fights over objects or attention.

- Dog is protecting something.

- Dog considers small, fast-moving objects — like children — as prey.

Begging, thieving & garbage gut

How many times have you heard, "My dog's a garbage dump," or "My dog's a Hoover?" Believe me, this is nothing to be proud of. Begging is not cute: at its best, it's plain unappetizing — who wants a drooling, sad-eyed mutt coveting the food on the table with a fixed stare? At its worst, begging — and getting — the wrong kinds of food (like chocolate) can seriously damage your dog's health.

The bare bones on begging

- *If begging is never rewarded, your dog will never beg.*
- If begging works some of the time, your dog will beg all of the time.
- Don't give your dog a treat for no trick. She'll learn begging is the trick.
- Don't let your dog be your baby's vacuum. She'll learn baby food = dog food.
- Establish regular feeding times so that your dog is not anxious about hunger.
- Throw unwanted or stale food in the proper receptacle. Your dog is not a garbage can.

Avoid freebies

Cuddles, attention, touch and treats must be earned. This does not mean that you should deny your dog the good things in life. It means that you discourage begging by ensuring that all treats and perks are earned. Unless Bandit is truly earning a treat, he shouldn't get one.
No trick = no treat, otherwise begging becomes the trick you are rewarding.

Teach your dog to not beg

If you never reward begging, you will never have to teach your dog to not beg. If your dog has picked up this nasty habit from someone else, follow these steps to train her out of it:

1. Feed your dog separately from yourself. Do so in advance of your own mealtimes so that she is not waiting expectantly throughout your meal.

2. Have a leash on your dog as you go into the kitchen area to prepare a meal. If she begins to beg, scold her with NO BEGGING, then escort her to a spot other than the kitchen, tie her to it and give a command such as LIE DOWN. The kennel is the best spot since it is already a part of training, and the door can be closed, avoiding the need to tie her. Give her a chew toy or bone as a reward.

3. If she cries or protests, ignore her. Do not release her until after your meal is done and she is quiet. If she cries so loud you cannot stand it, go to her but escort her on-leash further away from you to a place where her cries will not bother you. She must learn that crying will not get her what she wants and will not gain her access to your supper.

4. Eventually, you will be able to command your dog to GO TO YOUR KENNEL. She'll race off and sit there till the meal is over and you release her with OK, COME and praise. Remember to release her after

your meal, or she will soon learn to determine for herself when it is time to come out, instead of waiting for your permission.

5. If she at any time tests you or creeps back into the kitchen, repeat the learning steps and kennel her behind a closed door or tie her for a few meals.

Theft

Have you ever turned your back just for a minute only to find that Bandit has snatched the main course off the counter? Teach your dog DOWN, the rules of OFF and to respect the kitchen area. If you've done all that and he still steals, plots or connives to snatch your dinner, then try the following.

1. Plan to do this when you are in the mood to deal with your dog.
2. Rent a movie you have already seen.
3. Prepare the "bait." Try a pizza box with a bite-sized piece of pizza inside. Chances are you'll know what will tempt your dog.
4. Rig the bait. Attach tin cans or anything else you can think of so that when your bait is moved, you'll hear it.
5. Set the bait and wait.
6. When you catch your culprit, scold him and then kennel him for a half hour or so. *Only scold your dog if you catch him in the act.*
7. Re-set the bait. This time put lots of hot sauce on it.

Water fight

Many trainers recommend spraying a dog with water when he steals or misbehaves. If you are able to catch your dog in the act of stealing and spray him with water the first couple of times he tries to steal, this method will probably work by teaching him that stealing = unpleasant water spray. However, if your dog learns from experience about the kind of bootie that careful stealing can bring, he will probably learn only that he should not steal when you are present and armed.

8. Release your dog from the kennel with commands like SIT, COME, LIE DOWN — he must earn his freedom and praise.

9. Repeat steps 1 to 8, sometimes with nasty bait and sometimes with real bait so that your dog gets used to the idea that you will always catch him when he steals.

10. Never leave your dog unsupervised near food he cannot have until he is theft-free for at least six months. Kennel or confine him outside the food area if necessary.

Garbage gut

Fowl treats

Turkey, chicken or rib bones can be dangerous to your dog. They may splinter and cause serious injury. Never give these to your dog as a treat, and keep foraging under control.

This can be a very difficult problem to get rid of. People will often complain that walking their dog is like walking a Hoover, cleaning the park carpet of all the food debris. Certain breeds have very strong drives to scavenge and forage, and will find food, or objects they consider food, almost anywhere. Rather than fight this habit, try working with it: allow your dog to find and retrieve food, then teach him to bring, drop and earn praise plus a treat in response. This — together with teaching your dog to obey COME and HEEL — will rule out some of the irritations and dangers of your dog's scavenging habits.

1. Teach your dog FETCH, first with a toy or ball. Start in a confined area or on a long leash so that it is easy to enforce FETCH.

2. Throw the ball and command FETCH THE BALL.

3. When he runs and fetches it, command BRING THE BALL. Make your dog follow through on BRING using a second toy to tempt him.

4. When he brings the toy , command DROP. Show him the second toy to tempt him to comply. When he is playing consistently by the rules of FETCH for at least two weeks, start with two kinds of food: a not-so-tempting bone and a very tempting treat.

5. Using the FETCH command, throw a bone. Use a toy to tempt your dog to follow through on BRING.

6. Once he is close, show him your food reward and demand DROP.

7. If he drops, grab the bone, pick it up, command him to SIT and then give him the treat.

Refer to the "Games" section (page 113) for more elaborate instructions for FETCH.

When your dog has learned the basics and responds well to BRING and DROP, and has learned that he cannot eat everything he finds, you are ready for more objectionable canine candies. A different strategy is called for with untouchables like horse manure and rotting mushrooms:

1. Start on leash, scolding him as he bends to eat these forbidden fruits.

2. Command KEEP WALKING as you tug the leash and jog quickly past the tempting matter.

GOOD DOG!

The garbage instinct

The breeding of dogs has been done to select looks, abilities and behavioural traits. Sometimes a desirable trait like gentleness is inextricably linked to an undesirable trait like foraging. Two examples of this sort of genetic plus and minus are retrieving dogs and hound dogs. Retrieving dogs have had the kill instinct bred out of them so that they will carry prey shot by their masters without further harming it. With the kill instinct gone, all of the dog's diet must then be supplied by foraging, and presto, you have a very proficient garbage raider. With hound dogs, the highly powerful nose and tracking abilities make this dog aware of every discarded lunchbag and food remnant for miles.

3. Gradually expose your dog to more difficult-to-resist temptations like trails with manure and mushrooms. Keep your dog on a long leash to enforce the command.
4. Don't forget to reward him once in a while with treats.
5. When he automatically kicks into a trot upon hearing KEEP WALKING, let the leash trail as you walk and give commands as before.
6. Once he is reliably jogging past piles of poop, remove the leash. If he disobeys, revert back to on-leash drills.

While all puppies instinctively chew objects, there is no reason for them to chew your furniture, rugs, clothes and other valuables. Puppies can learn which objects they are allowed to chew and which they are not. Most puppies will stop destructive chewing if consistently caught, scolded, redirected and then praised.

For example, if your puppy is chewing a rug, the puppy should be:

- Picked up firmly.
- Scolded.
- Told, GET YOUR TOY, while you place the toy in the puppy's mouth.
- Praised when he chews the toy.

This puppy has learned that:

- Chewing the rug = bad attention.
- Chewing the toy = good attention.

In order for this method to work, your puppy cannot have access to forbidden items in your home when unsupervised. Also, you must be careful with what you consider a toy; don't give your puppy old shoes to chew on — he won't be able to distinguish old from new and will soon happily munch on your good pairs.

Some puppies seem to want to get caught. This is because they are hungry for attention and have learned that bad behaviours get more attention than good ones. Scolding

Puppy-proofing

Puppies, like small children, need extra protection. They are naturally inquisitive, and this can lead to serious injury. Make sure your house is puppy-proofed before bringing your new baby home. Electrical cords can be particularly dangerous, as can some common houseplants (see page 139), a fireplace, a swimming pool, and any small thing that a curious pup might be inclined to ingest. Items such as cigarette butts, elastic bands, balloons, sewing needles, thread, string or ribbon can be a lot more troublesome to get out than get in.

should last only seconds, while play and praise with a toy should last minutes. Make sure that you *always* redirect the negative behaviours. Scolding alone will have no effect. Your puppy must chew — he is driven by instinct. Scolding him for chewing the rug will only work if he is given something else that he is allowed and encouraged to chew. Otherwise the message you are teaching him is "don't chew," which is impossible to learn. Teach him instead to chew his toys and nothing else.

A brief note about kids, dogs and games

If you have kids, they will need suggestions and demonstrations from you on how to play these games. First work on the games without your kids present. Gradually have your kids join in the games by mimicking your command words or saying them with you.

Kids and dogs can make the best of friends, but they can also be a danger to one another. It is important that children learn that they either behave properly with their dog or they will not be allowed to play with her. Goldie will need a safe place to go when she has reached her limit, such as her kennel. Kids must be told that when Goldie runs to her kennel, this means she wants to be left alone, and must be left alone. Without a safe retreat, Goldie becomes a risk — even the sweetest Golden Retriever will bite or threaten kids if cornered and afraid.

Kids' rules

1. No hitting, smacking, play-fighting or pushing the dog.
2. No teasing, scolding or kicking the dog.
3. No wrestling or tug-of-war with the dog.
4. No chasing the dog when she runs away and hides or goes to her kennel.
5. No tail-grabbing or pulling.

Dog's rules

Goldie must also learn that playing with kids is a reward for her. If she breaks the rules, then she must be kenneled. The separation is the punishment, which teaches Goldie that if she can't play nicely, she can't play with kids.

1. No nipping, biting, jumping or chasing.
2. No aggressive growling, snarling or barking.
3. No "can't catch me," or tug-of-war (they encourage aggression and violence).
4. Always SIT when commanded.
5. Always respect BE NICE, NO, DOWN, OFF and GENTLE.
6. Always obey TIME OUT. Teach TIME OUT as a game in itself (see page 124).

Woof! Let the games begin!

Fetch

Always play FETCH with two toys that Bandit loves. Bring three if you think one might get lost. Start in the house with a small puppy or in the yard with an untrained dog.

How to play

1. Command FETCH THE BALL as you throw the ball.
2. Command BRING THE BALL once he has it in his mouth and turns to show you. Slap your side for emphasis.
3. When he is directly in front of you, say DROP as you hold your hand up high to show him the second ball.
4. Scoop up the first ball, praise him with GOOD BOY and throw the second ball, keeping one ball at all times.

Repeat steps one to four over and over and over and over.

If your dog has been taught to hog the ball, leash him on a long rope and practice until he has learned the new rules.

Fetch with a young puppy

Start with simple throws, rolling the ball past the puppy slowly. Note that puppy vision is not sufficiently developed to track fast-moving objects.

Advanced Fetch

Work on FETCH in new environments, such as water if your dog likes to swim, or in off-leash play areas. For athletic gotta-run dogs, use a tennis racket to hit the ball for a supreme workout. Eventually phase out the second ball. Continue to mime the action of lifting your arm as you command DROP. Keep an extra ball with you at first in case he refuses to drop without it.

Dos & don'ts of fetch

Do make sure that games are fun and last only as long as Goldie is interested and energetic.

Do be careful to not over-excite or push her past her limits

Don't allow FETCH to ever become "chase me" or tug-of-war. The only ball game you must ever play with Goldie is FETCH, or FIND & FETCH. Ignore her if she tries to bait you into a "chase me" game.

Find & Fetch

Once your dog has learned FETCH and enjoys retrieving her favourite toys, you may begin to use them as FIND & FETCH tools. You can also teach her FIND with food treats.

How to play

1. Make Goldie SIT and STAY with a human friend holding her in place.
2. Praise her for her SIT-STAY.
3. Let her watch you as you hide the prize.
4. When you're ready, release her with OK, FIND THE TREAT.

Start with hiding spots she can see, making it more difficult as she gets better at the game. Eventually, when Goldie has learned SIT-STAY, try to play this game without someone assisting you. Insist she wait and not start her search until you release her. As she gets quicker at finding the treat, make the hiding spots trickier and further away, but only in areas she is allowed to visit. Let her enjoy a few chews or bounces with the reward before you call her, praise her and start again. Keep a second toy handy for calling her, using the same method as in the return part of FETCH to guarantee a good DROP response.

Hide & Seek

Players: two people and Goldie. Goldie is always "it."

How to play

1. Start in your yard or house.
2. Hold Goldie on leash, or by the collar if you have full control.
3. Start with Goldie in SIT at your side.
4. Have a friend ("Amanda") approach and receive a dog treat from you.
5. Instruct Amanda to walk several steps away, then to stop and turn around.
6. Command Goldie, GO FIND AMANDA. Release her as you say this, and walk her to Amanda. Amanda should hold the reward so Goldie can smell and see it.
7. When Goldie goes for the reward, praise her and have Amanda give her the treat as she touches her.
8. Phase out the leash when Goldie is responding every time.
9. Once she has learned to find Amanda without fail, teach her to find a new person.

Set up again with Goldie in a SIT at your side and repeat the game. Each time she successfully finds and touches Amanda, she must be praised and given the treat. Gradually get Amanda to go further and further. Eventually get her to hide and have them truly play Hide & Seek.

Rules:

- Goldie must never hide, because that is no fun.
- Once the FIND command is given, it must be enforced so that your dog will take this command seriously — your dog may save someone's life someday. Leash and control your dog through the FIND search if necessary.

Come relay

Players: two people and Goldie

Goldie is required to SIT-STAY until released from the person she is with and called by the second player. She must then run from the first person to the second and stop and SIT-STAY at the second person's side. To a spectator this game looks like a game of catch where the two people are exchanging a dog instead of a ball.

How to play

1 Player One, holding Goldie on leash or by the collar, commands her to SIT and STAY. Player One must insist that Goldie STAY until giving the release words, OK, GO. Make sure to give the release before Player Two calls Goldie or she will learn to ignore SIT-STAY.
2 Player Two calls Goldie, gesturing wildly or slapping her thigh for emphasis. Use a ball or squeaky toy to tempt her if necessary. When Goldie comes, touch her, praise her and reward her with a few chews on the toy, as you hold her near you.
3 Once Goldie has responded, Player One should collect her again and set up to repeat the trick. When Goldie is a pro at this, have her run from Player One to Player Two and back again directly.
4 As Goldie improves, increase the distance between the players.

SIT, GOLDIE ... STAY

OK, GO.

COME GOLDIE!

Touch Goldie ... GOOD GIRL.

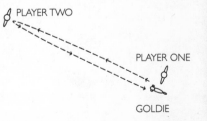

PLAYER TWO

PLAYER ONE

GOLDIE

123

Time Out

It is useful to teach TIME OUT as a separate game. Eventually, the command can be used during all games to ensure that play never gets too rough. If you teach it right, your dog will think of TIME OUT as a game, and gladly obey the command at any time.

1. Start with your dog on leash. Jump or jog around your dog, telling him PLAY as you do so.
2. After several seconds, say TIME OUT as you choke up on the leash and pull your dog's head down to the ground so that he lies down.
3. Lie down with him the first few times, and praise him. This looks like a "hit the dirt" army drill or a children's game of freeze tag.
4. Once your dog understands the trick, do it during leash walks, and reward it with a treat.
5. Whenever you say TIME OUT, you must enforce and praise it.
6. Once your dog understands the concept, take him off the leash and work on TIME OUT in the house, then the yard, then eventually in off-leash areas, at first on-leash and then off-leash with rewards.
7. Begin play again by releasing him with OK, PLAY.

This command is especially useful for families with children of varying ages and strengths. No matter how wild the game, if TIME OUT is enforced and rewarded every single time in the learning phase, your dog will always want to respond.

THE FINAL BARK

All dogs want to be good dogs, but most need to be shown how. A dog learns best when she is motivated by clear rules and praised as a reward. Stage exercises so that success is guaranteed. Begin in environments with low or no temptations, gradually increasing the distractions as she responds reliably to commands. Whenever your dog is disobedient or lazy, scale back to an easier situation and enforce simple commands. Make sure you give commands only when you are prepared to enforce them. Otherwise, your dog will think ignoring you is okay. Keep training positive by ending each segment with success and a reward. Take a lot of breaks and make play, cuddles and touch part of the reward.

Always praise good behaviour. Redirect bad behaviours by giving clear and direct commands, enforcing them with praise. Focus on the positive with attention, time and touch as a reward. For defiant or repetitive disobedience, isolate your dog so that she learns that she must obey your commands to earn your company and her place in the house.

Try not to expect too much. Allow your dog to learn at her own pace. Add new commands and tricks only after she has mastered the old ones. Trying too much too fast is a surefire recipe for failure. In a typical training session, your dog will work for four to five minutes, then earn breaks and cuddles. The entire time she is training, she

Avoid freebies

Whatever else you do, avoid freebies. If a dog gets everything she wants and needs for free, she will have no reason to obey commands. She will be convinced that she is already being a good dog since she is rewarded so often.

An exercise plan

Exercise is vital to your dog. He cannot be good — no matter how much he might want to be — if he is bursting to get out and run. Dogs are made to travel large areas and lead active, outdoor lives. Even the smallest of pooches needs a good work-out every day. Before you spend a lot of time and money on correcting behavioural problems and bad habits, give your dog the work-out he needs, each and every day. Give him the chance to be good.

should hear a command word once, then be guided through the correct response and rewarded. Should she disobey, scold her briefly before redirecting her behaviour and praising her. Through this style of training your dog learns how to be a good dog and will naturally be a healthier, happier dog.

A HEALTHY, HAPPY DOG

It is amazing to me how many people will splurge on doggie treats and toys, yet scrimp on doggie health care. Dogs don't always exhibit obvious signs of pain so you can't expect your dog to tell you when he needs to see the vet. The best strategy is to develop a good relationship with a veterinarian and visit every year. Choose a clinic that is conveniently close to you and friendly. Make sure you feel comfortable with the style of the office and the attitude of the staff. It may seem costly to pay for vaccines and other precautionary measures, but it is nowhere near as costly as treating the horrible illnesses these measures prevent. If cost is a major factor, use your telephone to shop around and find the best prices, or try your local S.P.C.A. hospital. Most dog illnesses are preventable — protect your dog.

In an emergency, you will want your dog to be comfortable and relaxed when you take him for treatment. The only way to achieve this is to bring your dog to the vet regularly, even when no treatment is necessary. Make sure the visit is positive, with treats and praise, and start as early as you can. Touch your dog often — especially on his paws and near his mouth, ears and tail — so he will tolerate touch.

I've asked Dr. Jack Brondwyn of Arbutus West Animal Hospital in Vancouver to provide me with some necessary health care measures a caring owner will provide throughout a dog's life. Keep in mind that

GOOD DOG!

injuries and accidents are bound to happen. Pet insurance plans are available, but as only undiscovered illnesses are covered, sign up when your dog is young and fit. Familiarize yourself with the illnesses and weaknesses of your dog and be alert in observing signs of those problems should they appear. Ask your breeder or vet for details. An ounce of prevention is always worth a pound of cure, and it can save a lot of heartbreak and suffering.

Healthy puppies

Bring your pup to the vet for a full examination at eight weeks of age. You may be required to bring a stool sample — ask your vet if anything extra is required. You will have at least two follow-up visits for booster shots and vaccines. It is extremely important to follow your vet's schedule as well as her instructions regarding when it is safe to expose your pup to other animals.

Ask your vet about specific problems you should watch for with your breed and size of dog and in your geographic location.

Adult dogs

Dogs need a booster shot every year, although vaccination protocols are often changing. Again, consult with your own vet for the best preventative program for your dog.

Ask your vet

Every region has its special dangers and preventative measures. In most of North America, heart worm is a serious problem requiring blood tests and pills — one per month throughout high-risk seasons. Lyme disease from ticks is another common, regional problem with a yearly preventative vaccine. Again, be sure to get details about your neighbourhood from your neighbourhood vet. It is also a good idea to consult with your vet about potential problems if you are travelling with your dog to another part of the country.

If fleas are a problem in your area, or if your dog is particularly sensitive to them, ask your vet about a flea program. It is definitely worth the cost on the flea-ridden west coast, and will save your dog from great discomfort and the potential for other, more serious problems.

Flea cycle facts

It is said that cockroaches will inherit the earth. I think it will be a close battle between cockroaches and fleas. Fleas can reproduce at an astonishing rate — each female can easily lay 2,000 eggs which can all be hatched within three weeks, and of course they too can lay eggs, and so on and so on.

What does not kill fleas: soap, water, washer and dryer, scrubbing, shaking, bathing, powders, garlic, flea collars, most flea sprays.

What does kill fleas: spray that is made to kill fleas, larvae and eggs, and flea dip bath products used by veterinarians and groomers

Spraying Bandit is not enough. You must spray the carpets, curtains, bedspreads and of course all of Bandit's favourite hangouts. If fleas are a problem for you, ask your vet about a special flea program designed to remove your dog's name from the flea Best Host list.

Six to nine-month old male

The sooner a male dog is neutered, the better. If you are not in a position to breed your male dog (and guarantee homes for all his offspring), then keeping him intact, with his strong drives to reproduce, will cause him stress, and his stress will cause you problems.

An unneutered male will be driven to seek out mates. He will escape, wander, fight and mate. He will be far more likely to get hurt in traffic since he will want to be out on the make, cruising the streets. He will be more likely to get into a fight since his scent will provoke aggression from other dogs — vet bills for one bite wound can be twice the cost of a neuter. A neutered male is also less prone to certain health complications, specifically prostate problems.

Six-month old female

Female dogs have two heats each year, lasting approximately three weeks. There may be obvious physical signs such as bloody discharge or a swollen vulva, but often there are none in young dogs. Expect bizarre behaviour from both the female in heat and from all other dogs around her. Unwanted escorts will accompany you on your walks and cry at your fence. Dogs will fight for her. She will flirt, spin, turn and rub.

A spay can be performed on an adult dog,

but is less traumatic on a pup. Even though you think your puppy is still a baby, in reality most female puppies come into heat between six and eight months of age and can get pregnant at this time. Many S.P.C.A. or Dog Rescue programs provide a spay/neuter certificate for all dog adoptions, reducing the cost dramatically. And the cost of a spay or neuter is nowhere near the cost of a litter and all the hassle and cleaning that goes with it. As well, if you spay your female dog before her first heat, you are protecting her against developing certain types of tumours.

Hospital time for a spay or neuter is usually half a day. Recovery time is two to three days, but your dog must remain quiet and clean because of the stitches. A bell collar will prevent your dog from removing the stitches when you can't be watching. Your vet may use dissolving stitches; if not, a follow-up visit to have the stitches removed should happen ten to fourteen days after the surgery.

LIFE CYCLE

A dog's life cycle and life expectancy varies according to breed and size. Generally, small breeds have longer lives, while large and extra-large breeds have a shorter life expectancy. Your dog's needs will change according to its own life cycle. Again, you should pay attention to any messages that your dog may be trying to give you about his changing needs, and don't be afraid to talk to your vet about any of your concerns.

VISIT YOUR VET

If your dog shows any unusual symptoms or abnormal behaviour, call your vet immediately and get advice. What may appear to be a minor irritaion could be an indication of something more serious. Don't take chances with your dog's health.

First aid kit

Dying for chocolate

Chocolate can be dangerous to your dog. It contains theobromine, a powerful stimulant that is toxic to dogs. Other sweets and desserts can also upset a dog's system, and cause serious health problems. Treat your dog with healthy snacks and lots of attention.

You should keep a dog first aid kit handy in case of emergencies. Make sure you have essential items such as gauze, bandages, clean water and a bowl, as well as the phone number and address of a twenty-four hour emergency vet clinic and the local poison control centre. A muzzle is a good idea because, if your dog is injured and in pain, you may have to muzzle him in order to treat him or move him. Your own vet can supply a list of other first-aid essentials, and provide advice on their use. In all emergencies, it's best to consult before giving treatment — the wrong treatment could make things worse.

Common poisons

Many items found in and around our homes and yards are deadly to your pet. The best thing to do, of course, is to prevent your dog from coming into contact with these poisons. If your dog is behaving strangely, or if you suspect that he may have ingested some toxic substance, get him in for treatment immediately. Some of the more common household items that can kill your dog are:

- antifreeze (a nontoxic antifreeze is available, but most varieties are highly toxic to dogs and cats, and the sweet taste is appealing)
- petroleum products
- most common household cleaners
- slug bait
- chocolate
- tylenol, and many other common or prescription medications
- rat poison
- pesticides or insecticides
- some common house plants, including deiffenbachia, lilies, philodendrons, azalea, ivy, amaryllis and spider plants. Ask your vet for a complete list.

A review quiz for you and your family

1. The dog trainer's most powerful tool is:
   a. Punishment.
   b. Scolding.
   c. Isolation.
   d. Praise.

2. Punishment works if used only when:
   a. The dog is bad.
   b. The dog is noisy.
   c. The dog isn't listening.
   d. The dog is caught in the act.

3. Command words should be used when:
   a. You want your dog to obey.
   b. You are able to enforce your commands.
   c. Your dog is misbehaving.
   d. Your dog is tempted to disobey.

4. The easiest way to house train a dog is:
   a. Paper train.
   b. Kennel train.
   c. Combination of paper and kennel training.
   d. Having your dog learn by himself.

5. Use the kennel or confined space:
   a. To punish your dog.
   b. To isolate and control your dog when unsupervised.
   c. Only when you go out.
   d. Only when your dog is very bad.

6. When your dog starts responding to training:
   a. Stop using the kennel.
   b. Be more lenient and flexible.
   c. Gradually increase freedom.
   d. Teach her new things.

7. Once your dog has learned the training basics and performs reliably:
   a. Stop training.
   b. Scale up temptations and teach new tricks.
   c. Allow total freedom.
   d. Give him less attention than when he was untrained and poorly behaved.

8. When your dog relapses and misbehaves:
   a. Ignore her if it happens only once in awhile.
   b. Re-direct her to behave and take away freedom.
   c. Punish her.
   d. Yell at her.

9. What behaviour should you pay the most attention to?
   a. Good behaviour.
   b. Bad behaviour.
   c. Aloof behaviour.
   d. Clingy behaviour.

10. What do you do if you call your dog and he doesn't come?

   a. Walk briskly the other way.
   b. Follow him.
   c. Stand still and yell.
   d. Stand still and talk baby talk.

11. What do you do if your dog won't heel?
   a. Walk her anyway.
   b. Stop walking her .
   c. Use a collar that gives you the control you need to enforce a heel.
   d. Get someone strong to walk her .

12. What is the correct way to give the COME command?
   a. GOLDIE, COME … touch … GOOD GIRL.
   b. COME … touch … GOOD GIRL.
   c. COME … COME … (repeat till she comes) … GOOD GIRL.
   d. COME ON … COME HERE … GOOD GIRL when she gets near.

13. If your dog starts to forget commands, tricks or rules you should:
   a. Punish him.
   b. Increase lesson time.
   c. Go slow and repeat old lessons with patience.
   d. Give up — he's stupid.

14. Treats should be given when the dog:
    a. Is cute or sweet or good.
    b. Is responding properly to a command.
    c. Is in the right place at the right time.
    d. All of the above.

15. The best way to stop a dog from jumping up is to:
    a. Knee her in the chest.
    b. Yell and scream and make a fuss when she jumps.
    c. Allow it when she's little and stop it once she grows.
    d. Ignore the jumping, and redirect her to SIT with praise.

16. Your dog understands that a rule is absolute when:
    a. It is enforced 100% of the time.
    b. It is sometimes enforced.
    c. It is enforced when people are around.
    d. It is almost always enforced.

17. If your dog is a noisy barker, you can teach QUIET by:
    a. Yelling, "Shut up."
    b. Giving him whatever he wants.
    c. Isolating him for barking and releasing him for quiet.
    d. Holding him.

18. If your puppy chews and destroys things, you must:

    a. Scold her.
    b. Catch her in the act and scold her.
    c. Ignore it because she'll outgrow it.
    d. Catch and scold her in the act, then redirect her to chew one of her toys.

19. If your dog bites your kids you must:
    a. Scold him.
    b. Catch him in the act and scold him.
    c. Catch him in the act and then isolate him.
    d. Ignore it — he'll outgrow biting.

20. If your dog won't return a fetch toy:
    a. Chase and play on her terms.
    b. Ignore her.
    c. Outsmart her to get the toy.
    d. Use a second toy to tempt her to return the first toy.

The answers, of course, are in the book.

Sirius Books

Sirius is the name of the most dominant star in the constellation **Canis Major.** Also known as the **Dog Star,** it is the brightest star in the entire night sky. **Sirius Books**, an imprint of **Polestar Book Publishers**, is a brilliant collection of books for **dog lovers**. Like a good dog, a Polestar book makes an ideal companion.

Polestar publishes a wide range of books, including fiction, poetry, children's fiction, sports books and innovative non-fiction. Our books are available at your favourite bookstore. For a complete list of our titles, contact us at:

Polestar Book Publishers
Second Floor
1011 Commercial Drive
Vancouver, British Columbia
Canada V5L 3X1
(604) 251-9718
Fax (604) 251-9738

SIRIUS BOOKS